Think-Alongs™
Comprehending As You Read
Level C

Steck-Vaughn

Program Authors

Senior Author
Roger Farr

Co-Authors
Jennifer Conner
Elizabeth Haydel
Bruce Tone
Beth Greene
Tanja Bisesi
Cheryl Gilliland

STECK-VAUGHN
ELEMENTARY · SECONDARY · ADULT · LIBRARY

A Harcourt Classroom Education Company

www.steck-vaughn.com

Acknowledgments

Editorial Director	Diane Schnell
Project Editor	Anne Souby
Associate Director of Design	Cynthia Ellis
Design Manager	Ted Krause
Production and Design	Julia Miracle-Hagaman
Photo Editor	Claudette Landry
Product Manager	Patricia Colacino
Cover Design	Ted Krause
Cover Sculpture	Lonnie Springer
Cover Production	Alan Klemp

Think-Alongs™ is a trademark of Steck-Vaughn Company.

ISBN 0-7398-0085-X

5 6 7 8 9 0   PO   03 02 01

Contents

What You Already Know

Read the story below. As you read, think about what you already know.

Lori could hardly wait for the school bell to ring. She was going shopping after school. She was going to buy a gift for her best friend. She had been saving her money. Lori hoped she had enough to buy the gift. It was for her friend's birthday. What a surprise it would be!

When you read the story, you probably thought about many different things. Check the boxes next to what you thought of while you read.

This story made me think about a gift I bought for a friend.

I thought of

☐ a time when I could hardly wait to do something.

☐ a time when I saved money to buy something.

☐ another story in which someone saved money.

What else did you think of while you read?

_____

_____

_____

_____

Read and Think

- Read the selections that follow.
- Stop at each box and answer the question.
- Remember to think about what you already know.

The Paper Bag Princess

By Robert N. Munsch

This selection is about a princess named Elizabeth who tries to save Prince Ronald from a dragon. Read the selection to find out whether Elizabeth is able to save Prince Ronald.

Elizabeth was a beautiful princess. She lived in a castle and had expensive princess clothes. She was going to marry a prince named Ronald.

Unfortunately, a dragon smashed her castle, burned all her clothes with his fiery breath, and carried off Prince Ronald.

 1   What other stories does this story remind you of?

Elizabeth decided to chase the dragon and get Ronald back.

She looked everywhere for something to wear, but the only thing she could find that was not burnt was a paper bag. So she put on the paper bag and followed the dragon.

He was easy to follow because he left a trail of burnt forests and horses' bones.

Finally, Elizabeth came to a cave with a large door that had a huge knocker on it.

She took hold of the knocker and banged on the door.

2 What do you think might be in the cave?

The dragon stuck his nose out of the door and said, "Well, a princess! I love to eat princesses, but I have already eaten a whole castle today. I am a very busy dragon. Come back tomorrow."

He slammed the door so fast that Elizabeth almost got her nose caught.

Elizabeth grabbed the knocker and banged on the door again.

The dragon stuck his nose out of the door and
said, "Go away. I love to eat princesses, but I have
already eaten a whole castle today. I am a very busy
dragon. Come back tomorrow."

"Wait," shouted Elizabeth. "Is it true that you are the smartest and fiercest dragon in the whole world?"

"Yes," said the dragon.

"Is it true," said Elizabeth, "that you can burn up ten forests with your fiery breath?"

"Oh, yes," said the dragon, and he took a huge, deep breath and breathed out so much fire that he burnt up fifty forests.

3 Tell about someone you know who is like Elizabeth.

"Fantastic," said Elizabeth, and the dragon took another huge breath and breathed out so much fire that he burnt up one hundred forests.

"Magnificent," said Elizabeth, and the dragon took another huge breath, but this time nothing came out.

The dragon didn't even have enough fire left to cook a meat ball.

Elizabeth said, "Dragon, is it true that you can fly around the world in just ten seconds?"

"Why, yes," said the dragon and jumped up and flew all the way around the world in just ten seconds.

He was very tired when he got back, but Elizabeth shouted, "Fantastic, do it again!"

So the dragon jumped up and flew around the whole world in just twenty seconds.

When he got back he was too tired to talk and he lay down and went straight to sleep.

Elizabeth whispered very softly, "Hey, dragon." The dragon didn't move at all.

She lifted up the dragon's ear and put her head right inside. She shouted as loud as she could, "Hey, dragon!"

The dragon was so tired he didn't even move.

Elizabeth walked right over the dragon and opened the door to the cave.

 4 Describe a time when you had to be very brave.

There was Prince Ronald.

He looked at her and said, "Elizabeth, you are a mess! You smell like ashes, your hair is all tangled and you are wearing a dirty old paper bag. Come back when you are dressed like a real princess."

"Ronald," said Elizabeth, "your clothes are really pretty and your hair is very neat. You look like a real prince, but you are a bum."

They didn't get married after all.

5 In what ways is Elizabeth not like other princesses?

Time to Write!

At the end of the story, Elizabeth decides that she is not interested in Ronald anymore. Imagine that you are Elizabeth. Ronald asks you why you became angry with him.

• For this activity, you will write what you would tell Ronald about why you are upset with him.

Prewriting

First, think about how friends should treat each other. Write how friends should behave and how friends should not behave.

How should friends behave?

_____

_____

_____

_____

How should friends not behave?

_____

_____

_____

_____

Writing

Now, use another sheet of paper to write what you would tell Ronald.

13

Elsa's Pet

By Maureen Ash

This selection is about a girl named Elsa who wants to have a pet. Read the selection to find out about Elsa's new pet.

"You could get a fish," said Elsa's mother. Elsa knew that her mother was trying to help, but that old answer wasn't any help at all. She was allergic to all the good pets, like cats and dogs.

"The fun part about a pet," Elsa said, "is holding it and petting it. I can't pet a fish."

1 What are some reasons it is fun to have a pet?

14

"No, not without scaring it," agreed Elsa's mother. "I wish I could help you." She took a bucket from under the sink and wrinkled her nose. "Ick," she said. "Will you take this out to the compost pile, please? It's pretty smelly."

Outside, Elsa dumped the bucket of food scraps onto the compost pile. Something moved on the ground. Elsa squatted down and saw—a worm. It was moving toward a pile of old leaves and grass clippings. As the front end of the worm stretched forward, the worm became long and skinny. Then the worm became shorter and fatter again as it drew its tail end forward.

2   What are you thinking about now?

Elsa gently picked up the worm. She held it in front of her face, examining the pink skin and the pattern of rings around its body.

"Hi, worm," Elsa said. "Do you want to be my pet?"

In the house, Elsa placed the worm on a piece of white cardboard. She ran to get her magnifying glass. Peering at her new pet, she saw it raise one end. It seemed to look around.

3   What do you know about worms?

"Do worms have eyes?" Elsa asked.

"No, they don't," answered her mother. "Worms can only feel."

"It has a nose!" exclaimed Elsa. "It has a little nose that sticks out in front."

"A nose? I don't think so." Elsa's mother looked through the magnifying glass. "Hmmm," she said. Then she took a book from the shelf. She found a picture and showed it to Elsa.

4 If you wanted to learn more about worms, what would you do?

"That looks like a nose to me, too. But this book says it's a pad of flesh that covers the worm's mouth. When the worm is searching for food, the pad is stretched out. And when it finds food, the pad pulls the food into the worm's mouth and closes over it."

"It's hungry!" exclaimed Elsa. "Let's make a home for it and feed it."

Elsa's mother helped Elsa put some soft dirt into a plastic box for the worm.

"What does it eat?" Elsa worried. "I don't want it to starve."

"It won't starve." Elsa's mother brushed dirt from her hands. "Worms eat organic matter."

"Where do we buy that?" Elsa asked.

"Organic matter is stuff that is alive or was alive," Elsa's mother explained. "The potato skins and carrot peelings and dead leaves that we put in the compost pile are all food for worms."

 5   What are you thinking about now?

"Worms eat that stuff?"

"They do," answered Elsa's mother, "after it gets soft from being wet and starts to rot. The worm takes in the organic matter for food. Then the waste comes out the tail end of the worm and makes wonderful fertilizer for our garden. You can even buy it at the garden store—it's called earthworm castings. We'll just mix a few rotten vegetable peelings into this soil, and your worm will have plenty of food."

"Yuk," said Elsa. "It might be better to eat dirt."

 6 What do you think about eating dirt?

"Well, worms do eat some dirt. They don't have teeth for chewing, so they need the dirt to help them grind the organic matter into small bits. Then their bodies can absorb it. This grinding happens inside the worm, in its gizzard."

"Birds have gizzards, too," said Elsa.

"That's right," said Elsa's mother.

"And birds eat worms! Our worm is lucky to be away from the robins, right?" asked Elsa.

"Yep, I guess so," her mother answered. "Remember when we saw that robin pulling the worm?"

"Yes," said Elsa. "It was a tug of war."

"Look." Elsa's mother showed Elsa the picture in the book. "See how the worm looks like a lot of rings stuck together? Each of those rings has tiny bristles, called setae. Those bristles are the reason the robin had to pull so hard to get that worm. The setae help the worm hold on tight to the earth when it is partly in its hole. The setae also help the worm crawl forward. And as the worm moves through the soil, it loosens the soil, so air and water can get down to the roots of plants."

"That's another reason we like worms in our garden, right?"

Elsa thought about all the worms she'd seen last summer when they dug up their potatoes.

"You bet," said Elsa's mother. "We like worms."

Elsa petted her worm very gently, placed it in its box, and watched it wriggle its way underground.

---

7   In what ways would a worm not make a good pet?

Time to Write!

Elsa and her mom learned about worms as pets. It is important to know about an animal as a pet. Imagine that you have a friend who wants to get a pet.

- For this activity, you will write to your friend about an animal and why this animal would be a good pet.

Prewriting

First, use the space below to help plan your response.

What animal should your friend get for a pet? _____

```
┌──────────────────┐                    ┌──────────────────┐
│                  │                    │                  │
│                  │                    │                  │
│                  │                    │                  │
└──────────────────┘                    └──────────────────┘

┌───────────┐      ┌──────────────────┐      ┌───────────┐
│           │      │  Why this animal │      │           │
│           │      │  would make a    │      │           │
│           │      │  good pet        │      │           │
└───────────┘      └──────────────────┘      └───────────┘

┌──────────────────┐                    ┌──────────────────┐
│                  │                    │                  │
│                  │                    │                  │
│                  │                    │                  │
└──────────────────┘                    └──────────────────┘
```

Writing

Now, use another sheet of paper to write to your friend about the animal.

Rocco's Yucky

By Linda Crotta Brennan

Let's Read

This selection is about a boy named Rocco. He wants to teach his friends how to make gnocchi (NYUH kee). Read the selection to find out what gnocchi is.

Rocco rolled the clay long and thin. Amanda looked at it. "Are you making a snake?" she asked.

"No, I'm making gnocchi," said Rocco.

"What?" asked John, looking up from his clay monster.

"I'm cooking gnocchi," said Rocco. He cut the clay into pieces that looked like little pillows.

"Yucky?" asked Amanda.

"Boys don't cook," said John.

"My father likes to cook," said Rocco. He pushed his thumb into each pillow of clay. "And when we make gnocchi, everybody helps."

 1   What do you think gnocchi might be?

Say NYUH kee.

"Yucky?" said Amanda again.

"Not yucky," said Rocco. "Gnocchi."

John laughed and danced around the classroom. "Yucky, yucky. Rocco cooks yucky!"

When he got home, Rocco slouched in his chair at the kitchen table. "John says boys don't cook."

His father laughed. "How's this for boy cooking?" He gave Rocco a taste of the tomato sauce he was making.

"It's good," said Rocco, but he didn't smile. "The kids at school said gnocchi was yucky."

"No one who ever ate gnocchi would think it was yucky," said his father.

That gave Rocco an idea.

"Good thinking," said his father when Rocco told him about it. "I'll call your teacher right now."

2 What are you thinking about now?

The next morning Rocco carried a big box to school. "Rocco has a surprise for us," his teacher told the class.

Rocco took flour, cold mashed potatoes, eggs, and a bowl out of the box. He propped up a sign with a recipe. On the top it said GNOCCHI: POTATO PASTA.

Rocco measured the flour into a big bowl.

"Let me break the eggs!" said Amanda.

John added the mashed potatoes. Rocco sprinkled in some water.

Everybody mixed and kneaded the dough. Then they rolled it into wiggly snakes.

"Hey, cooking is fun," John said.

 3 What do you know about cooking?

They cut the dough into pillows.

"Make a thumbprint in each one," said Rocco.

Then they sprinkled the pillows with flour.

"Now we let them dry overnight," said Rocco.

Amanda rubbed her tummy. "I can't wait."

GNOCCHI: POTATO PASTA

The next day the teacher boiled some water in a big pot. Carefully she put in the gnocchi and let them boil until they floated to the top of the water.

Rocco served the gnocchi with his father's tomato sauce and some cheese.

"Mmm-mm," said the teacher.

John licked his lips. "And I helped cook!"

"This is yummy," said Amanda. "Why do you call it yucky?"

Rocco rolled his eyes. "It's not yucky," he said. "It's gnocchi!"

4　What are you thinking about now?

Time to Write!

Rocco taught his friends how to do something new. What could you teach your friends?
- For this activity, you will write directions that tell how to do something.

Prewriting

First, list the materials you need. Then, list the most important steps to follow.

What do you want to teach your friends to do?

_____

What materials do you need?

_____

_____

_____

What steps should be followed?

_____

_____

_____

_____

_____

Writing

Now, use another sheet of paper to write directions that tell how to do something.

Thinking About

How Things Are Alike and Different

Read the story below. As you read, think about how things in the story are alike. Also, think about how they are different.

My father and my stepmother both work. My father paints houses. My stepmother is also a painter. She paints pictures. People buy her paintings for their homes. My father has to leave our house when he paints. My stepmother paints at home.

I also want to be a painter when I grow up. I just have to decide one thing. Do I want my work to go on the inside of people's houses, or on the outside?

Did you think of things that are alike and different as you read this story? Answer the questions below.

This story makes me think of different kinds of painting.

How are the father and the stepmother in this story alike?

_____

_____

How are they different?

_____

_____

What else did you think of while you read?

_____

_____

_____

_____

Read and Think

- **Read the selections that follow.**
- **Stop at each box and answer the question.**
- **Remember to think about how things are alike and different.**

Whales: The Gentle Giants

By Joyce Milton

Let's Read

This selection is about whales. Read the selection to learn how whales are alike and different from other animals that live on land and in the sea.

Some whales are as big as small islands. The blue whale is the biggest of all whales. The blue whale is also the biggest animal in the world. A baby blue whale is even bigger than an elephant.

There are about seventy-five different kinds of whales. The sperm whale has a huge head. The male narwhal has one long, twisted tooth. Sometimes this tooth grows to be ten feet long! The pygmy sperm whale is one of the smallest whales. It is about the size of a canoe. That's still pretty big!

1 How are whales different from one another?

People used to think that whales were a kind of fish. But a whale is not a fish. It cannot stay underwater all the time. A whale breathes through a hole in its head. This is called a blowhole. When a whale dives, it holds its breath. When it comes up, it breathes out. A big spout of spray comes out of its blowhole. Up it goes, high in the air.

 2 How are whales different from fish?

A whale is a mammal. Just like a dog. Just like a cat. Just like you! A baby mammal grows inside its mother's body.

This baby gray whale has just been born. Its mother and another whale quickly push the baby to the top of the water. They are helping the little whale take its first breath of air.

The baby whale is called a calf. It drinks its mother's milk just as a human baby does. It weighs about 2,000 pounds. But to its mother it is still her little baby.

3 How are whales like land animals?

Usually whales are gentle. But not always. The mother gray whale will fight anything that tries to hurt her calf. The whale calf cannot swim very fast. A big, hungry shark is watching. It is waiting for a chance to attack. But the mother whale is keeping watch too.

When she sees the shark, she rushes straight at it. Other whales come to help. They swim between the shark and the baby. They are too big for the shark to attack. The shark is not very smart. Soon it is all mixed up. It gives up and swims away. The calf is safe.

4 How are whales smarter than sharks?

All winter long the baby gray whale swims and plays in the warm waters off the coast of Mexico. But when spring comes, the gray whales are on the move. They will swim all the way to cold Arctic waters. Even the baby whale will make the long trip.

They swim day and night. But sometimes even a whale gets tired. When the whales are sleepy, they lie on top of the water and take naps.

5 How do whales sleep differently from how you sleep?

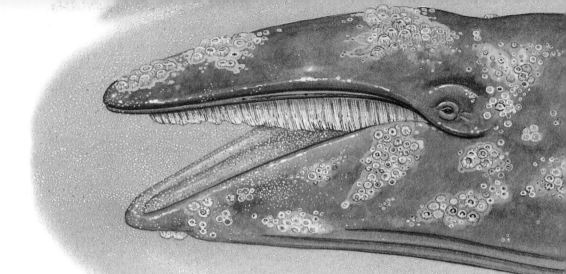

After their long trip the gray whales are very hungry. The cold water is filled with their favorite food—tiny sea animals, so small you would not think they could feed a whale. But they do. The whales open their mouths wide. SLURP! They take in lots of water. And *lots* of tiny sea animals too.

Like many whales, the gray whale has no teeth. Instead it has baleen. The baleen grows in long strips. It works like a big strainer. When a whale spits out a mouthful of water, lots of the tiny sea animals stay caught in its baleen. They will be the whale's dinner.

People did not always know that whales make sounds. Sailors in submarines used to hear strange things: CLICKETY-CLICK! CRRRACK! The noises sounded like music from outer space. The sailors were surprised to learn that all those sounds were made by whales.

Humpback whales make the strangest sounds of all. They seem to be singing. Humpbacks are funny looking. Their heads are covered with bumps. But the songs they sing are beautiful. Scientists have even recorded the songs of the humpbacks. What do the songs mean? So far scientists are not sure.

6   What have people learned about whales?

The most beautiful whale is the black-and-white orca. The orca does not have baleen. It has real teeth—big ones! The orca hunts big fish. It hunts seals, too. It even hunts other whales. Orcas are also called killer whales. Sailors used to be afraid of them.

Today we know that orcas can become very tame. Orcas are the stars of many aquarium shows. They like to be petted. They love to do tricks. Orcas are very smart. Sometimes they even make up tricks and teach them to their trainers.

7 How are orca whales different from other whales?

Orcas do not hunt people. But for many years people hunted whales. Why? Mostly they wanted the whales' blubber. Blubber is a kind of thick fat. It can be made into oil. Years ago whale oil was burned in lamps. That's how people lit their houses.

Ships spent many months at sea looking for whales. The hunters searched for whales in the cold seas of the far north. Sometimes the ships got stuck in the ice. Some never returned.

Hunting whales was dangerous work. When they found a whale, the hunters chased it in small boats. They threw long spears called harpoons into the whale's back. The whale fought hard to get away. A frightened whale could overturn a boat!

So many whales were killed that few were left. People started to worry about saving the whales. Laws were passed to protect whales. Today most people who follow whales only want to watch them.

 8 Why do people today not need whale oil?

Scientists watch whales to learn about their lives in the sea. Whale watching is also fun. Whales seem to like watching people, too. They will swim and play around a boat for a long time. If you go whale watching, you might even see a whale jump high in the air. Why do whales jump? No one knows. Maybe they jump just because it feels so good to be a whale!

9 How do people treat whales differently today than they did many years ago?

Time to Write!

You found out from the selection that whales and fish are different. You want to share what you learned with your classmates.

• For this activity, you will write a report explaining how whales and fish are alike and how they are different.

Prewriting

First, use this chart to show how whales and fish are alike and how they are different. The first two facts are done for you.

Characteristic	Whales	Fish
They live in water.	yes	yes
They come to the surface to breathe.	yes	no
Their babies are born alive.		
They drink their mother's milk.		
They are hatched from eggs.		
They are very good swimmers.		
They hold their breath underwater.		
They stay underwater all the time.		

Writing

Now, use another sheet of paper to write your report about how whales and fish are alike and different.

41

Diego Rivera: An Artist's Life

By Sarah Vázquez

Diego Rivera was a famous Mexican artist. During his life, he tried many different painting styles. Read the selection to find out about the different painting styles he used.

Diego Rivera was born in 1886 in a town called Guanajuato. It is high in the mountains of Mexico. Diego had a twin brother named Carlos. His parents were very happy when the twins were born. Their other babies had died.

Diego Rivera was named after his father. His father worked as a teacher. He also visited other schools to make sure they were teaching the children well. Diego's parents helped poor people. His parents wanted everyone to have a better life.

1 How are Diego's parents like someone you know?

Diego loved toy trains. One of his favorite things to do was to take them apart. He wanted to see how trains worked.

Diego also loved to draw. He began drawing when he was just three. He liked to draw trains. He drew everywhere he could reach. He drew on the chairs, on the walls, on the floor, or on paper.

Diego spent much of his time drawing.
Sometimes he drew on the walls of his bedroom.
His parents didn't want him to draw there, so they
covered the walls in his room with plain paper. Then
Diego was free to draw on his walls. That is how he
painted his first wall paintings. These wall paintings
are called murals.

 2 How might painting a mural be more difficult than
painting a picture on paper?

Diego the Student

When Diego was ten years old, he started using paints to add colors to his drawings. Then he decided to be a painter. His parents let him take art classes after school.

After high school, young Diego went to the San Carlos School of Fine Arts. There he learned to love the art of the Mexican Indians. Their art showed the land, people at work, and their animals.

Diego learned many lessons from his teacher. Diego's teacher had a shop in Mexico City. He drew cartoons that made people laugh. He liked to draw poor people as being very good and rich people as being bad.

Diego began to paint this way, too. In 1906, some of his paintings were in an art show. He began to sell his paintings to earn money. His paintings sold well.

3 What are you thinking about now?

Diego the Painter

Diego Rivera wanted to learn more about painting. He went to Europe in 1907 to study. He tried many different painting styles. He liked paintings that showed real people in real places. He did not like the modern styles where things did not look real.

In 1921, Diego went back to Mexico. He painted a mural for a school. He showed many Indian people in this mural. He painted with bright, strong colors. The shapes were large and simple. This was his own style.

Diego also used many pieces of colored glass to make murals. They are called mosaic murals.

His Marriage

In 1928, Diego met an artist named Frida Kahlo. She was in art school, and Diego was painting a mural there. She went to see him about her paintings. They became friends and got married a year later. In the following years, they became famous together.

4 How did Diego's life and art change?

Frida had been in pain much of her life. Frida had polio as a child and was in a bus wreck in her teens. While she was ill, she taught herself to paint. She painted many self-portraits.

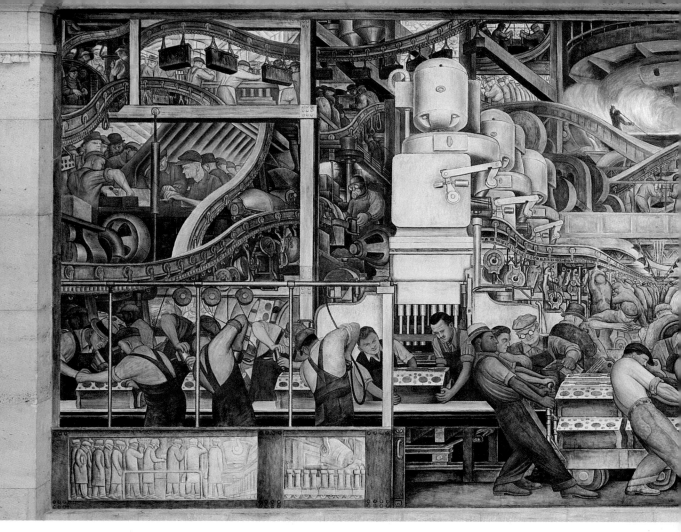

His Later Years

In 1931, there was an art show in New York City with 150 of Diego's paintings. Many other artists came to study with him. He became famous for his style of painting murals. He liked painting pictures that could be seen by many people in public places.

In 1932, the City of Detroit hired Diego for a huge job. He painted 27 murals on four walls of the Detroit Institute of Arts.

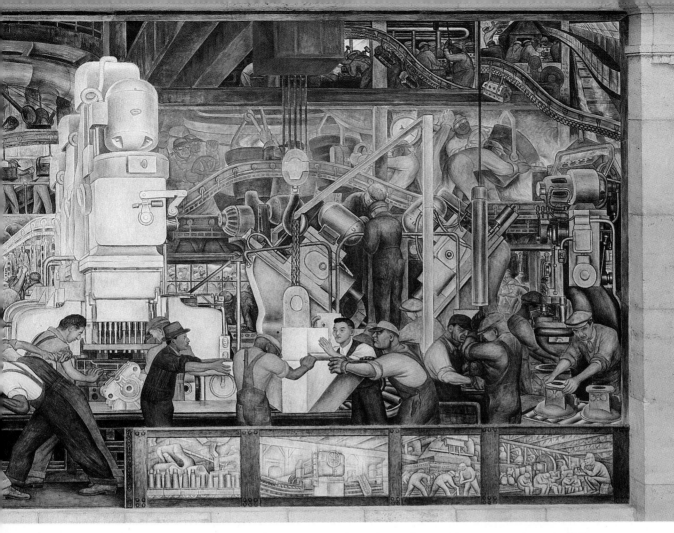

In 1933, Diego was hired to paint a mural by a man in New York City. But when the man saw the people in the mural, he did not like one person shown. He asked Diego to change it, but Diego would not. After Diego was paid, the man had the mural painted over. Later, Diego painted a smaller mural of this scene in Mexico City.

5   What are you thinking about now?

After that, Diego had hard times for a while. He lost some jobs in the United States. He didn't sell as much there. But he kept busy painting in Mexico.

In 1950, Diego Rivera won Mexico's National Art Prize. His country held a big party for him on his seventieth birthday. But in 1955, he became ill, and he died a year later.

Diego Rivera's art lives on. Many of his paintings and murals are in museums all around the world. Some of his best murals can be seen in the National Palace in Mexico City. Because of his beautiful artwork, people will always remember Diego Rivera.

Time to Write!

Diego Rivera grew up to be a famous artist. Imagine that your school is having a career day. You can invite someone to talk to your class about what they do.

• For this activity, you will write an invitation to someone to talk to your class on career day.

Prewriting

First, think of two different careers that interest you. List reasons you think you would enjoy each one.

Career 1:

_____

_____

_____

_____

Career 2:

_____

_____

_____

Which career do you think you would enjoy more?

_____

Writing

Now, use another sheet of paper to write an invitation to a person to talk about that career.

51

A Look at Spiders

By Jerald Halpern

Let's Read

This selection is about spiders. Read the selection to find out about different kinds of spiders. Also, find out how spiders are different from insects.

What Is a Spider?

Some people think that spiders are insects, but they are not. Both spiders and insects have a hard covering on the outside of their bodies. Spiders have eight legs and no wings. Insects have six legs and usually do have wings.

1 How are spiders different from insects?

All spiders have the same body parts. The main part of their body is divided into two sections. In the front, there are eight legs and two pinchers. Special parts in the back, called spinnerets, make silk. Spiders use the silk to make webs.

Spiders have five senses. Their sense of touch is the strongest. They can feel anything that moves near them. They use their mouth and front pinchers to taste and smell food. To see, most spiders have eight eyes. Spiders have small openings on their legs to help them hear sounds.

2 What are you thinking about now?

How Big Are Spiders?

Spiders can be very large. They can even grow bigger than an adult's hand. But spiders can also be much smaller. Some never get bigger than the top of a pin. Female spiders are always larger than male spiders.

Tarantulas are the largest spiders in the world. Those found in South America can be as long as a sheet of paper. Comb-footed spiders are the smallest spiders. They can be as small as the point of a pencil.

 3   How do spiders compare in size?

Where Do Spiders Live?

Spiders live in many places. They live at the top of mountains or on the bottom of caves. Some live in damp areas. Others live in deserts. Some spiders live on the ground, some in trees, and some in buildings.

The water spider lives in a pond. It makes a silk home on underwater plants. The spider traps a bubble of air and brings it below to its home. This is how the spider can breathe while in the water.

Most spiders live in silk webs they have built. Some webs have a round shape. Some webs have a zigzag look, and some look like tents. A spider's web is amazing to see.

4 What are different places spiders live?

How Do Spiders Make Silk?

Spiders make silk inside their bodies. It is squeezed out like toothpaste through the spinnerets. The silk is like thread that gets hard. Spiders use their silk in different ways.

Most spiders use their silk to weave a web. But not all spiders make webs. Some use silk to make a bed on a leaf. Others use silk to line tunnels in the ground. Many spiders use silk to wrap up insects so they can eat them later.

5   What different ways do spiders use silk?

How Do Spiders Eat?

Spiders have a strange way of eating. They turn their food into a liquid. Then they drink the liquid. It is like drinking milk through a straw!

Spiders are picky eaters. They usually eat only insects. Sometimes they may eat small frogs or lizards. First they trap the prey in their web. Then they poison it with a bite.

6 What interested you about the way spiders eat?

What Kinds of Spiders Are There?

There are many different kinds of spiders. Spiders can be different in color and in size. They can also be different in the ways they move and how they hunt for their prey.

Tarantulas are very large and hairy. They are the biggest of all the spiders. Tarantulas use sharp fangs to bite and kill their prey. They can also shed their long hairs to poison their prey.

Jumping spiders have short legs, but they are able to jump very far. Two of their legs are used just for jumping. These spiders jump to sneak up on insects. They jump again to catch them.

Trap-door spiders dig tunnels in the ground. They line the tunnels with silk they have spun. Then the spiders make a door made of silk and dirt. Trap-door spiders spend the day inside with the door closed. At night, they raise the door and go out to trap insects.

7 What are you thinking about now?

A wolf spider is a very good hunter. It has keen eyesight and is able to move quickly. During the day, the wolf spider searches for insects. When it sees one, it races up and catches it.

Crab spiders move sideways slowly, just like crabs do. Crab spiders often trap and eat bees and butterflies. Sometimes they can change their body color to match what is around them. This helps them catch their food.

 8 What different ways do spiders catch their food?

Can Spiders Harm People?

Few spiders are harmful to people. All spiders use their poison when they bite their prey. But their poison rarely harms people. Usually a spider bite just itches.

In North America, there are only six kinds of spiders that can harm people. The most dangerous is the black widow. This spider's poison is stronger than a rattlesnake's. The female black widow spider is the one that bites.

 9   What are you thinking about now?

If you find a spider, look at it carefully. Count its legs. See its colors. Notice its beautiful web. Spiders are very interesting to watch!

Time to Write!

Imagine that some of your classmates think spiders are insects. They think all spiders are the same.

- For this activity, you will write a story for your school newspaper. Tell how spiders and insects are different. Choose one spider and tell how it is different from other spiders.

Prewriting

First, list the ways spiders and insects are alike and different.

How spiders and insects are alike:

_____

_____

_____

How spiders and insects are different:

_____

_____

_____

A very unusual spider is _____ .

What makes this spider unusual?

_____

_____

Writing

Now, use another sheet of paper to write a newspaper story about spiders.

61

You have been thinking along as you read. Now practice thinking along to help you answer test questions.

Read and Think

- Read each selection.
- Stop at each box and answer the question.
- Answer the questions at the end of each selection.

Who is Shane?

Michael and Shane were never apart. Everywhere that Michael went, Shane was there, too.

Sometimes you would see Michael without Shane. Shane never came outside on rainy days. On partly cloudy days, he might come out. As soon as the sun disappeared, Shane was gone.

Michael liked Shane. He liked to play games, seeing how tall he could make Shane.

1 What are you thinking about now?

Sometimes, though, Michael got tired of Shane. It was worse than having a little brother. Every time Michael took a step, Shane took a step. Michael sat down to rest, and Shane would sit, too. When Michael played ball, Shane always had to get into the game.

Michael tried to leave Shane behind one day. But he could not get away. Shane flattened himself against the buildings and sneaked along.

One day Michael was on his way to the park. Shane was tagging along. It seemed as if they were sewn together at the feet.

2 What are you thinking about now?

Michael stopped to eat a frozen fruit bar. There was Shane eating one, too. Michael looked at his empty stick. It said, "You win a lucky wish!"

"Hooray!" Michael cried. "I wish that Shane would go home and stay!" He started off down the street. Soon he felt people looking at him. "Why are you staring?" Michael asked Ben and Ava.

"I'm not sure," Ben said, "but there's something strange about you today."

"Something's missing," Ava said, looking behind, beside, and in front of Michael. Ben and Ava left Michael to play alone.

Michael was lonely. He wished Shane were there to follow him when he danced down the sidewalk. He decided to go home and tell Shane he was sorry. Then he noticed a girl who looked very odd. She had two shadows, and one of them looked like a boy!

"Shane!" Michael cried. "Is that you?" It was, and Shane was happy that Michael had found him. The girl was very happy, too.

"That thing has been following us for an hour," she complained to her own shadow. It waved back at her. Michael took a huge step and a hop, checking to see that Shane was once again following along.

 3 What are you thinking about now?

Darken the circle for the correct answer.

1. **Michael can go outside without Shane on days when _____.**
   Ⓐ Shane is too tired to go
   Ⓑ there is a ball game
   Ⓒ Ben goes along
   Ⓓ the sun is not shining

2. **Michael got rid of Shane by _____.**
   Ⓐ sitting down to rest
   Ⓑ making a lucky wish
   Ⓒ sneaking away from him
   Ⓓ talking to Ben and Ava

3. **Where did Shane go when Michael sent him home?**
   Ⓐ to follow a little girl
   Ⓑ to play ball with Ben
   Ⓒ flat against the buildings
   Ⓓ to look for rain

4. **Shane is Michael's _____.**
   Ⓐ best friend
   Ⓑ brother
   Ⓒ shadow
   Ⓓ toy

Write your answer on the lines below.

5. **What happens in this story that could not really happen?**

_____

_____

_____

_____

Why are there falcons in our cities?

The peregrine is a kind of falcon. It had almost died off by the 1970s. There were only 39 pairs left. DDT was a poison that was used to kill insects. But the DDT stayed in the bodies of the small birds that ate the insects. When the peregrines ate the small birds, they also ate the poison. The poison made the shells of the eggs so thin that they broke. Also, horned owls were killing many peregrines. Scientists knew they needed to help the birds. They protected peregrine eggs until they could hatch. Laws were passed to stop the use of DDT.

1 What are you thinking about now?

About the same time, some of these large, beautiful birds moved into big cities. They began living on tall buildings. There were no owls to attack them there. DDT was not used there. There were many pigeons for them to catch and eat.

Scientists set special boxes on top of the buildings and put young peregrines in them. The scientists fed the birds, but the birds learned to catch food, too. A few landed in the streets, and people took them back up to their boxes.

The peregrines liked the city. They stayed there. Today they are flying around downtown Denver, New York, Baltimore, and other cities all over America. It is wonderful to look up at them soaring above the busy streets! The scientists did save the peregrines. Now there are 1,600 pairs!

2   What are you thinking about now?

Darken the circle for the correct answer.

6. A peregrine is a kind of _____.
   Ⓐ poison
   Ⓑ falcon
   Ⓒ owl
   Ⓓ scientist

8. Scientists might have to climb out on tall city buildings in order to _____.
   Ⓐ shoo the peregrines away
   Ⓑ save the pigeons
   Ⓒ help the peregrines
   Ⓓ clean the ledges

7. One of the problems for the peregrine was _____.
   Ⓐ the poison DDT
   Ⓑ tall buildings
   Ⓒ pigeons
   Ⓓ boxes

9. To the peregrine, the horned owl is _____.
   Ⓐ a friend
   Ⓑ a helper
   Ⓒ a good meal
   Ⓓ an enemy

Write your answer on the lines below.

10. How have scientists helped save the peregrines?

_____

_____

_____

Help Name the Person of the Year!

It is time to name Person of the Year! Will it be someone from your class? You can suggest, or nominate, anyone. Think of a student who has done many things for our school this year.

Rosalie Hernandez was Person of the Year last year. She got Trevson Tree Company to plant trees in front of the school. Rosalie also won the city spelling bee.

1 What are you thinking about now?

The same person cannot win two years in a row. So think of someone else to suggest this year. Here's what you need to do:

1. Get a nomination form from Mrs. Williams.
2. Name your choice for Person of the Year.
3. In 100 words or less, tell why that person should be Person of the Year.
4. Sign your name.
5. Turn in the form to Mrs. Williams by March 30.

You could become Person of the Year yourself, if someone else suggests you. Rosalie, Mrs. Williams, and Mr. Cookston will pick three persons from those you suggest. On April 14, all the students in the school will vote to decide who will be the Person of the Year.

2 What are you thinking about now?

Darken the circle for the correct answer.

11. One thing Rosalie did was to
_____.

Ⓐ get some trees planted

Ⓑ help Mrs. Williams

Ⓒ nominate a good friend

Ⓓ win the math contest

13. Who makes the final decision about who will be Person of the Year?

Ⓐ the whole school

Ⓑ the fifth graders

Ⓒ the students who were nominated

Ⓓ Rosalie, Mrs. Williams, and Mr. Cookston

12. What should you do if you want a friend to be Person of the Year?

Ⓐ enter the spelling bee

Ⓑ talk to Rosalie

Ⓒ fill out a form

Ⓓ pick three persons

14. If you want to become Person of the Year, you need to _____.

Ⓐ get a friend to turn in your name

Ⓑ plant trees

Ⓒ nominate yourself

Ⓓ talk to Mr. Cookston and Rosalie

Write your answer on the lines below.

15. Why do you think the school has the rule that the same student cannot be Person of the Year twice?

_____

_____

_____

What Might Happen Next

Read the story below. As you read, think about what might happen next.

The night was stormy and cold. Amy's whole family was in the kitchen. The windows rattled every time the wind blew. Then there was a loud BOOM. The lights went out. Amy's mother lit a candle. Her father gave them flashlights. Then there was a knock at the door. A man told them, "There is a chance of flooding here. Please go to the school. Hurry!"

Amy's family quickly packed some things. They stayed at the school until it was safe to go home. Was their house flooded? They were glad to see that it was safe.

When you read the story, you were probably thinking what would happen next. Check the boxes next to what you thought of while you read.

This story made me wonder what would happen after the lights went out.

- [ ] I wondered if the wind would break a window.

- [ ] I wondered who knocked on the door.

- [ ] I wondered if Amy's house would flood.

What else did you think of while you read?

_____

_____

_____

_____

Read and Think

- Read the selections that follow.
- Stop at each box and answer the question.
- Remember to think about what might happen next.

Floss

By Kim Lewis

Let's Read

This selection is about a young sheepdog named Floss. Read the selection to find out the trouble Floss gets into and what she does next.

Floss was a young Border collie who belonged to an old man in a town. She walked with the old man in the streets and loved playing ball with children in the park.

"My son is a farmer," the old man told Floss. "He has a sheepdog who is too old to work. He needs a young dog to herd sheep on his farm. He could train a Border collie like you."

 1 What do you think is going to happen?

74

So Floss and the old man traveled, away from the town with its streets and houses and children playing ball in the park.

They came to the heather-covered hills of a valley, where nothing much grew except sheep.

 2 How do you think Floss will feel about working with the sheep?

Somewhere in her memory, Floss knew about sheep. Old Nell soon showed her how to round them up. The farmer trained her to run wide and lie down, to walk on behind, to shed, and to pen. She worked very hard to become a good sheepdog.

But sometimes Floss woke up at night, while Nell lay sound asleep. She remembered playing with children and rounding up balls in the park.

The farmer took Floss up to the hill one day to see if she could gather the sheep on her own. She was rounding them up when she heard a sound. At the edge of the field, the farmer's children were playing with a brand-new black-and-white ball.

3 Now how do you think Floss will feel about working with the sheep?

Floss remembered all about children. She ran to play with their ball. She showed off her best nose kicks, her best passes. She did her best springs in the air.

"Hey, Dad, look at this!" yelled the children. "Look at Floss!"

The sheep started drifting away. The sheep escaped through the gate and into the yard. There were sheep in the garden and sheep on the road.

"FLOSS! LIE DOWN!" The farmer's voice was like thunder. "You are supposed to work on this farm, not play!"

He took Floss back to the doghouse.

4 What do you think is going to happen to Floss?

Floss lay and worried about balls and sheep. She dreamed about the streets of a town, the hills of a valley, children and farmers, all mixed together, while Nell had to round up the straying sheep.

But Nell was too old to work every day, and Floss had to learn to take her place. She worked so hard to gather sheep well that she was too tired to dream any more. The farmer was pleased and ran Floss in the dog trials.

5 What do you think is going to happen to Nell?

"She's a good worker now," the old man said.

The children still wanted to play with their ball.

"Hey, Dad," they asked, "can Old Nell play now?"

But Nell didn't know about children and play.

"No one can play ball like Floss," they said.

So the farmer gave it some thought.

 6   Now what do you think is going to happen to Floss?

"Go on, then," he whispered to Floss.

The children kicked the ball high into the air.

Floss remembered all about children. She ran to play with their ball. She showed off her best nose kicks, her best passes. She did her best springs in the air. And they all played ball together.

---

7 What do you think Floss will do from now on?

Time to Write!

Floss has to work with the sheep every day. Floss wants some time to play ball. Floss likes to work, and she likes to play. Think about what you might like to do when you are older. What might you do for fun? What might you do for work?

• For this activity, you will write a journal entry about what you might do when you are older.

Prewriting

First, think about what you might do when you get older.
Think about what you might do for fun and for work.
List your ideas below.

Fun _____

_____

_____

_____

Work _____

_____

_____

_____

Writing

Now, use another sheet of paper to write your journal entry.

81

Gail Devers: A Runner's Dream

By Katherine Mead

You are about to read a true story. It is about a woman who always wanted to be the best at what she did. She had to get through some hard times first. Read the selection to find out how Gail Devers became a champion.

Becoming a Winner

Do you ever dream of being the best in the world at something? You might be the best singer, basketball player, or tennis player. What would you like to be?

This is the story of a woman who has always wanted to be the best. Gail Devers is a famous runner who trained many years to become a winner. She has won two gold medals in the Olympics. It was not easy for her to do this, but she kept trying until she did.

1 How do you think Gail Devers became a winner?

Gail Devers grew up in California. Her father was a minister, and her mother was a teacher's aide. Gail and her big brother liked to swim and ride bikes together. Gail loved to be active.

Gail was a good student. When she was in high school, Gail found something she was really good at doing. She could run really fast.

Gail's high school didn't have a track team. There was no one to teach her about running and winning races. She had to learn on her own.

Gail became a very good sprinter. A sprint is a short, very fast race. Gail's best sprint was the 100-meter dash. This is a little longer than a football field.

Gail also learned to run in races that have hurdles to jump over. Hurdles are gates about as high as a kitchen counter. A runner jumps over ten hurdles while sprinting as fast as she can.

Before long, Gail was racing against the best high school girls in the country. She was still training on her own, without a coach.

2   What are you thinking about now?

The Olympic Dream

Running was very important to Gail, but so was school. Gail wanted to be the best runner and the best student, too.

Gail became very good at both. She went on to college at the University of California. There she met the women's track coach, Bobby Kersee. He had coached some of the best women runners in the world.

Bobby Kersee knew that Gail could be a winner when he saw her race. He became her coach and her friend.

The same year that Gail started college, the 1984 Olympics were held in Los Angeles. Coach Kersee told Gail to watch the United States women's track team carefully.

"Why?" Gail asked.

"You are good enough to make the team in 1988," said Coach Kersee.

3 Do you think Gail is going to run in the 1988 Olympics?

Gail saw the great runners and wanted to be a part of the Olympics. She worked hard and won many races. In 1987, she ran the 100-meter dash in just under 11 seconds. That was close to a world record!

4 What are you thinking about now?

Coach Kersee was excited. "Once Gail sees what she can do, no one can stop her!" he said.

In 1988, Gail Devers was chosen for the U.S. Olympic team. She was making her dream come true. Gail wanted to show she was the best sprinter and best hurdler. But something was wrong.

Gail didn't know why, but she wasn't feeling her best. She was having a hard time running races. She was running slower than she had in high school. No one was sure what was wrong, but Gail didn't get any better. Gail found it was harder and harder to race.

5 Now tell whether you think Gail will run in the 1988 Olympics.

Gail Gets Sick

Gail got worse instead of better. Every race was harder than the one before. Soon she couldn't see with her left eye. She had headaches, she lost weight, and her body shook. Her doctors couldn't find out what was wrong.

Gail had to stop running. Her feet hurt her so badly that her family had to carry her around. But Gail never gave up hope. She studied hard and finished college at the University of California.

At last in 1990, doctors found that Gail had a serious illness called Grave's disease. Her doctors weren't even sure that she would live.

Gail's doctors found a medicine that helped her. By the spring of 1991, Gail began to feel better. She started to walk again. No one thought she'd be able to run. But Gail and Coach Kersee knew she would run again.

 6 What do you think will happen?

Gail came back one step at a time. First she walked, then she jogged in socks, and finally she ran. Under Coach Kersee's careful eye, Gail Devers began sprinting again. Some said it was a miracle. Gail said it was because she believed in herself. Coach Kersee believed in her, too.

The 1992 Olympic Games were one year away. It was a short time for Gail to get ready. She had to work very hard.

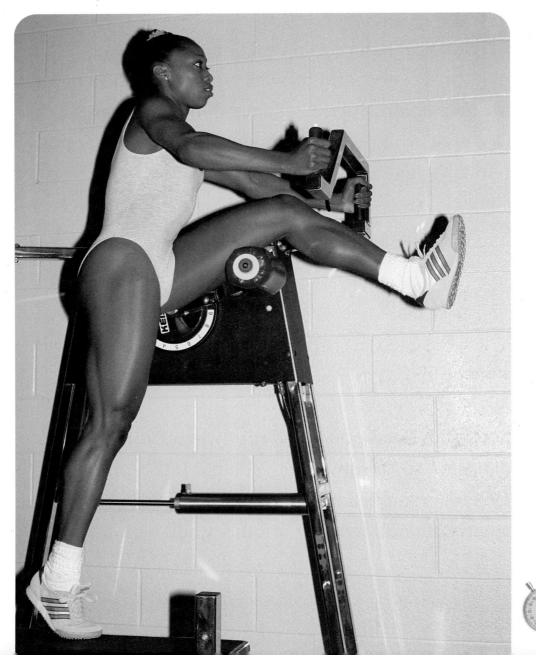

Gail knew she could make it. She took her medicine, rested, and ate well. Then she began to run in races again. Soon Gail won some big races. At the Olympic trials, Gail was great in the 100-meter dash and 100-meter hurdles.

7 What are you thinking about now?

Coach Kersee had said that when Gail made up her mind to do something, she did it. Gail made the 1992 Olympic team. She would go to Barcelona, Spain. She had reached another goal.

Going for the Gold

At the Olympics, Gail was set to run the 100-meter dash and the 100-meter hurdles. Everyone thought she'd win the hurdles.

People did not think she could win the 100-meter dash because she had been so sick. She surprised everyone. Gail ran her fastest race ever, with a time of 10.82 seconds. That's about how long it takes to start a car!

 8 What do you think Gail will do in her next race?

She won a gold medal. When she got her medal, everyone in the stadium stood up and cheered for her. Coach Kersee and Gail's family cheered the loudest. They knew she was a great hero.

Gail was hoping to win a second gold medal for the 100-meter hurdles. She thought this was her best race.

During the race, things didn't go the way she'd hoped. Gail started with a big lead. As she was about to cross the finish line, she tripped on the last hurdle. Four other runners came in before her. She didn't win, but she did finish the race. Gail said, "I'll be back next time. The word *quit* is not in my vocabulary."

9 What do you think Gail will do next?

In 1996, Gail Devers won another gold medal at the Olympics in Atlanta, Georgia. She had done it. She had become the best. Sometimes dreams take a little time to come true.

Time to Write!

Imagine that your friend wants to be the best at something. What would he or she need to do to become the very best?

• For this activity, you will write a letter telling your friend what he or she will have to do to become the very best.

Prewriting

Answer the questions below to help you plan your letter.

What goal is your friend trying to reach?

_____

What will you tell your friend is the most important thing to do?

_____

_____

What will you tell your friend to do when he or she does not win every time?

_____

_____

What will you tell your friend to do if he or she does not become the very best?

_____

_____

_____

Writing

Now, use another sheet of paper to write a letter to your friend who wants to be the best.

Abe Lincoln's Hat

By Martha Brenner

Let's Read

This selection tells about Abe Lincoln's life as a lawyer before he became president of the United States. Read this selection to learn some facts about the life of Abe Lincoln.

Abe Lincoln didn't have much money. But when he became a lawyer, he wanted to look his best. He bought a long black coat and a tall black hat. Every day Abe wore his hat to his new job. People noticed the tall man in the tall hat. He was friendly to everyone. When they needed a lawyer, they remembered him.

Abe lived in Illinois. His state was mostly wilderness. Then more and more settlers came. They built houses and farms and new towns.

Sometimes they didn't get along. They argued over land and animals and money. Lawyers like Abe could help people settle their arguments. They could help people get a fair trial in court.

1 What do you think this story will be about?

Abe Lincoln was a smart lawyer. People came to him with all kinds of problems. He helped them all. But he had one problem himself. He forgot to answer letters. He forgot where he put important papers. A good lawyer cannot forget. Abe wanted to be a good lawyer, but he was not a good paper-keeper. What could he do?

2 What do you think Abe could do?

Abe had an idea. His tall hat! He could push letters deep inside it. He could stuff notes into the leather band. When he took off his hat, the papers would remind him what he had to do. The idea worked, most of the time.

One day some boys played a trick on Abe. They tied a string across the street. They strung it way up high. Everyone in town could walk under it. Everyone except Abe.

When Abe walked down the street, the string knocked off his hat. Papers flew everywhere! He bent over to pick them up. The boys ran out of hiding. They jumped all over him. Abe laughed. He was not mad at the boys. He liked a good joke. But the trick did not stop him from carrying papers in his hat!

3 What are you thinking about now?

Once a lawyer sent Abe a letter. Abe stuck it in his hat. The next day, Abe bought a new hat. He put away his old one. Weeks later the lawyer wrote again: "Why didn't you answer my letter?" Then Abe remembered. The letter was still in his old hat!

Many towns in Illinois had no lawyers and no judges. So every spring and fall, a judge and some lawyers traveled from town to town. Abe went too. He packed his hat with papers, his checkbook, and a handkerchief.

At the head of the parade of lawyers rode the judge. No one could miss him. He weighed over 300 pounds. Two horses pulled his buggy.

Abe's horse was skinny and slow. His name was Old Buck. Abe and Old Buck traveled lonely country roads. In the snow. In the rain. In the mud.

4   What was Abe going to do when he traveled?

Traveling made Abe very tired. He dreamed of a soft bed and a good meal. But the lawyers had to stay at poor country inns. The food was bad. The rooms were cold. The beds were crawling with bugs. The lawyers had to share beds. Except the judge. He had his own bed.

5 What are you thinking about now?

Early in the morning the courthouse bell would ring. Abe hurried to court. Pigs lived under one courthouse. Abe had to talk loudly over the grunts and squeals.

People came from near and far to hear Abe. He made trials easy to understand. He told jokes and stories. People said he could make a cat laugh.

Once Abe whispered a joke to another lawyer. The lawyer laughed out loud. "Quiet!" the judge yelled. "You are fined five dollars." When the trial was over, the judge asked to hear the joke. He laughed as hard as the lawyer. "That was worth five dollars," he said. "Forget the fine."

At another trial two men argued over who owned a young horse. Each said he owned the mother of the colt. Abe led everyone outside. He put the two grown horses on one side of the lawn. He held the colt on the other side. Then he set the colt free. It headed straight to its real mother!

6 How did telling jokes and stories help Abe?

One day Abe got a letter. It was from Hannah Armstrong. Years before, Abe had lived with her family. Mrs. Armstrong cooked for Abe. She sewed up the holes in his pants.

Now she begged Abe for help. Her son Duff was in jail—for murder! Abe did not stick this letter in his hat. He wrote back right away: "Of course I'll help you."

Duff had been in a big fight. It was very dark. But a man said he saw Duff kill someone. Duff said he did not do it. Abe believed Duff. But how could he prove that the man was wrong—or lying?

 7   What will Abe do to help Duff?

"How could you see in the dark?" Abe asked the man.

"The moon was full," the man said. "It was bright as day."

"Are you sure the moon was full?" Abe asked again and again.

"Yes," the man repeated.

Then Abe held up a famous book of facts. It said there was NO moon in the sky at the time of the fight! Now no one believed the man anymore. The judge set Duff free!

Abe believed slavery was wrong. His state had laws against it. But the laws were not clear. Many blacks were treated like slaves. Nance was one of them. She worked for a storekeeper who sold her to another man. This man treated Nance badly. So she would not work for him.

Abe argued for Nance in court. Illinois was a free state, he said. All its people are free, whatever their color. The judge decided Abe was right. From then on, no one could be bought or sold in Illinois.

Abe had saved Nance. But half the states in America still had slaves. In a few years there would be new states out west. Abe did not want slavery to spread to these states.

Abe tried to get elected to the U.S. Senate. If he won, he could make laws to stop slavery. He ran against Stephen Douglas. Douglas argued that each state should decide for itself if it wanted slaves. They gave speeches all over Illinois. Thousands of people heard them. Abe lost the election but became famous.

 8 What do you think Abe will do next?

In 1860, Abe ran for president. Stephen Douglas ran too. This time Abe won.

Abe grew a beard for his new job. He took his family to Washington. At every train station, crowds cheered the new president.

Abe was ready to make his first speech as president. He carried a cane, a tall silk hat, and his speech. He looked for a place to put his hat.

Stephen Douglas stepped up. "If I can't be president," he said, "I can at least hold his hat."

Abe Lincoln was a great president. He freed the slaves. He worked for fair laws. He helped unite the nation after a long war. But he never changed his ways. He always kept important papers in his tall hat!

9 What are you thinking about now?

Time to Write!

Imagine that your class is writing a book about different presidents. You have been asked to write a chapter about Abe Lincoln. Include information about what Abe Lincoln did that made him so interesting.

- For this activity, you will write a chapter about Abe Lincoln.

Prewriting

Use the idea web below to help plan what you are going to include in your chapter.

Facts About Abe

Writing

Now, use another sheet of paper to write your chapter about Abe Lincoln.

What Could and Could Not Really Happen

Read the story below. As you read, think about what could really happen and what could not happen.

Lee woke up and looked at the clock. "Oh no," he thought. "It is already after 8:00!" He jumped out of bed. "School started at 8:00," he thought. "I hate to be late." He put on his school clothes. He ate breakfast. He brushed his teeth and combed his hair.

Then he walked outside. His dog, Spot, was waiting out front. "Don't worry," Spot said. "I have already set the time machine to get you to school on time." Lee and Spot set off in the time machine toward school.

What could have really happened? What could not have happened?

Put a ✔ beside what could have happened.

Put an ✖ beside what could not have happened.

This story made me wonder if a time machine could really work.

☐ Lee used a time machine to get to school on time.

☐ Lee brushed his teeth and combed his hair before school.

☐ Spot is a dog that can talk.

☐ Lee woke up late for school.

What else did you think of while you read?

_____

_____

_____

_____

Read and Think

- Read the selections that follow.
- Stop at each box and answer the question.
- Think about what could and could not really happen.

Wilbur Meets the Thing

By Caroline Coderre

This selection is about Wilbur, who gets scared at night. Wilbur decides to find out what is making the noises he hears when he is tucked in bed. Read the selection to find out what Wilbur hears.

Wilbur was scared.

He was tucked safely into bed for the night, and all was dark and cozy.

But . . .

"Mom!" Wilbur called. "There's something out there!" His eyes were round with fear.

1 What does Wilbur think is out there?

"Nonsense," said his mother. "You're imagining it. Go to sleep."

Wilbur huddled deeper in bed and pulled his blanket up to his chin. He was sure he could hear the thing out there moving.

"Mom," he called again. "It's still there. I can hear it."

"Really, Wilbur," his mother said, sighing. "I told you, you're imagining things. There's nothing there. Now please be quiet and go to sleep."

2 If you were Wilbur, what would you say to your mother?

"I wish she'd believe me," Wilbur grumbled to himself. "It's not fair. That thing is out there every night, keeping me awake. If I could catch it, then Mom would HAVE to believe me."

Wilbur grabbed his fishing net. With his furry, green hand he pushed open the door of the closet where he lived. "Here goes!" he thought.

 3   What just happened?

"Grroarr!" roared Wilbur as he leaped out into the middle of the bedroom.

"Eek!" yelled the child on the bed, sitting up.

"Aak!" yelled Wilbur. "You scared me."

"YOU scared ME," cried the girl. "I knew there was a monster in the closet. Mom didn't believe me."

4   Draw a picture of Wilbur and the thing that he heard outside of his bed.

"My mom didn't believe me either," said Wilbur. "What's your name?"

"Lisa," said the girl. "You don't look so scary close up. Your fur looks soft."

"My name's Wilbur," said the little monster. "You're not as big as I thought."

"Do you eat people?" asked Lisa.

"No!" cried Wilbur. "Yuck! I like peanut butter sandwiches, apples, bananas, things like that. I hate spinach, though."

"Ugh. Me, too," said Lisa. "That's a nice fishing net you have."

"You could borrow it sometime," offered Wilbur.

"Do you sleep in my closet?" Lisa asked.

"Every night," said Wilbur. "I'm sorry I scared you."

5   How is Wilbur like other monsters? How is he different from other monsters?

"I'm sorry I scared you, too. I'd better go to sleep now. See you tomorrow?"

"I'll be here," said Wilbur. "Shall I tuck you in?"

Wilbur smoothed the covers over the little girl. Then he bent down and kissed her cheek. "Good night," he said.

"I'm glad you sleep in my closet," said Lisa. "It's nice to have a friend close by in the dark."

"Yes, it is," said Wilbur. Then Wilbur the monster went back into the closet, and Lisa the little girl snuggled down under the covers, and they both went to sleep.

6 Would you like to have Wilbur live in your closet?

Time to Write!

"Wilbur Meets the Thing" is fun to read. It is a story with a twist. Now, you are going to write your own story.

• For this activity, you will write a story including things that could and could not really happen.

Prewriting

First, think about what you are going to write. Who will the characters in your story be? What will happen in your story?

Draw a picture of a character in your story.

About my story character: _____

_____

What happens to my story character: _____

_____

_____

Writing

Now, use another sheet of paper to write your story.

113

Save the River!

By Sarah Glasscock

Let's Read

This selection is about a boy named Vince. He lives in the future with his computer named Jane. They go back in time to help save a river. Read the selection to find out how they try to save the river.

A River in Trouble

It was the year 2097. Vince was floating on his back in the clear water of the San Carlos River. His computer named Jane was waving from the shore.

1 What do you think about a computer that can wave from the shore?

"Jane, would you show me what this river looked like one hundred years ago?" Vince asked.

"Sure. Why do you want to see it as it was back then?" asked Jane.

"I'd just like to know if the river was this beautiful then," said Vince.

2   What are you thinking about now?

Soon Jane's screen lit up. There was a picture of the river as it had looked one hundred years ago. Jane made the picture bigger so Vince could see it.

Vince looked closely and saw a man and his son fishing. "Maybe that's my great-great grandfather!"

Jane quickly searched her computer memory. "That could be. You did have relatives here at that time."

"There were so many animals that came to the river back then," Jane said. "The San Carlos has been giving them food and water for hundreds of years."

A few feet away, Vince saw a deer drinking from the river. "It still does. The river hasn't changed. That's amazing. I wonder why the river hasn't changed."

A message popped up on Jane's screen from May 5, 1997. It said, "Help us save the river! Lina and Al." The words kept flashing on the screen.

"Jane, we have to do something!" said Vince. "Since you and I can travel back in time, let's go back and help them."

3   What books or movies does this remind you of?

Jane agreed that they should travel back into the past and see the river as it was back in 1997.

Jane sent a message to get the time machine. Suddenly the Time Traveler, a big bubble ship, floated down to the ground. "Get ready for a trip, Jane. Let's travel back in time to the year 1997," said Vince.

"If we go back, we can't change things ourselves," Jane reminded him. "We can only help Lina and Al."

Vince said, "I know, but let's try to help them." Vince and Jane changed into 1997 clothes and got into the Time Traveler. Then it rose into the sky and began its journey back in time.

Vince and Jane to the Rescue

The Time Traveler landed by some homes near the San Carlos River. But the year was 1997! Vince and Jane heard some voices outside. They peeked out and saw a girl and a boy talking to a woman. Jane quickly did a computer check on them. "It's Lina and Al!" Jane said.

4 What do you think Vince and Jane are going to do?

The woman was saying, "I don't agree with you. I don't want to give up my green grass and flowers. I don't want to see dried up grass when I look at my yard!"

Lina said, "Mom, if we use too much water, the San Carlos River could dry up someday." Lina's mom pointed the hose at her car to wash it.

Al pointed to some bags of lawn food. He asked, "Mrs. Reyna, are you going to put all that on your lawn?"

"Yes, green grass needs lots of food and water," Lina's mom said. "It doesn't grow on its own. I'm just trying to make our home look beautiful. Don't worry so much. Nothing bad is going to happen to the river."

"But the lawn food goes into the ground, and it ends up in the river," Al said.

"And the soapy water from the car ends up in the river, too," Lina said.

"What do you want me to do?" Lina's mom asked. "Drive a dirty car? Kill the grass? Let the weeds grow? I really don't think I'm polluting the river."

5 What do you think about what is happening to the river?

"We could take our car to a car wash that uses very little water," Lina said. "And our lawn doesn't need tons of water either, Mom."

"You're our mayor," Al added. "People will listen to you if you ask them to start SAVING water."

"You could ask people to work to keep the river clean," said Lina.

Mrs. Reyna aimed the hose at her car. "I'll think about it. You two go and play. Have some fun."

Lina and Al left and started walking down the sidewalk. Vince and Jane ran to catch them. They knew no one would understand that they had come from the future. So they had to act like they were from 1997.

6 What are you thinking about now?

Vince said, "Hi. We got the message you sent about saving the river."

"How did you get it?" asked Al.

"We saw it on our computer. We want to help you save the San Carlos River," Vince added. "How can we help you?"

Lina shook her head. "Thanks, but I don't know. We're having a hard time getting people to listen to us. They can't see what they're doing to the river."

"What if people could see what they are doing to the river?" asked Vince. "They may not believe you now, but we could show them proof. Let's get some water from the river and put it in these jars. Then anyone will be able to see that the river water is dirty. We'll take the jars to a TV station. We can ask if they'll do a news story about the river."

"Wow, then people really will see what they're doing to the river. This idea might work," said Lina and Al.

"Then we could ask people to call the mayor with ideas about saving the river," Vince added.

"She's my mom," Lina said. "We're trying to think of a way to get her to change her mind. She thinks nothing bad will happen to the river."

"If enough people call, maybe she'll change her mind," said Vince. "It's worth a try."

They ran to the river with the jars. Vince filled them with some dirty river water. Then he put the lids on tightly.

 7 What do you think about their plan to save the river?

The Mayor's Turn

Mayor Reyna was working in her office at the city hall. People had been calling her all morning. Jim Reed from the TV station was coming to talk to her.

Someone had put a jar of dirty water on her desk. Mayor Reyna held the jar up to the light and looked at the dirty water. The label on the jar said, "San Carlos River."

The mayor's aide, Bev, walked into the office. "Did you see this article in the newspaper today? It's about how dirty the water is in the San Carlos River. Everybody wants to talk to you about it," Bev said.

"Good," the mayor said with a smile. "I have a lot to say about it. Call the newspapers and the TV stations. Call Lina and Al, too. Ask them to come over. They'll be surprised at what I have to say."

8 What do you think the surprise will be?

Many people came into the mayor's office. Mayor Reyna held up the jar of dirty water. "This is water from the San Carlos River. Would you drink this water? Would you swim in it? We must stop polluting this river now."

The mayor went on, "This is what we need to do. We'll do three things:

1. Conserve our water.
2. Stop polluting.
3. Learn to take care of the river.

I'm sure I can count on all of you to help save the river." Everyone clapped after the mayor's speech.

Vince and Jane said good-bye to Lina and Al. Then they sneaked back to the Time Traveler. It was time to go back to the future, to the year 2097. Vince said, "I'll miss Lina and Al. I think we helped them at just the right time."

Suddenly, a message trailed across Jane's screen. It said, "WE DID IT! Lina and Al."

 9   How can you tell whether this was a true story or not?

Time to Write!

Vince and Jane went back in time to help save a river. You know that problems cannot be solved with help from the future.

• For this activity, you will write a letter to the mayor about a problem in your city. Tell how you can help solve the problem.

Prewriting

First, name three problems. Tell how you can help solve them.

Problem: _____

_____

How I can help solve the problem: _____

_____

Problem: _____

_____

How I can help solve the problem: _____

_____

Problem: _____

_____

How I can help solve the problem: _____

_____

Writing

Now, choose one of the problems.
Use another sheet of paper to write
a letter to the mayor about it.

Some Jungles Are Noisier Than Others

By J.R.M. Vance

Let's Read

Have you ever wondered why some animals look the way they do? This selection tells how tigers might have looked. Read the selection to find out how tigers got their stripes.

Long ago, tigers were not covered with a coat of stripes. No, back then tigers were covered with small metal pipes. I know that sounds silly, but it's true. Those pipes made an awful noise, clattering and clanging throughout the jungle. The tigers were not happy about their coats, but they did not know how to change them.

1   What do you think about tigers with pipes?

One day a young tiger decided that he had had quite enough of his coat of pipes. He went deep into the jungle, and he found Sahr, the Giver of Large-Cat Coats.

"Hello," said the tiger. "My name is Tonga, and I would like to have a coat that is not covered with pipes."

Sahr blinked the sleep from his eyes. "I really can't see what I can do for you. Things are the way they are supposed to be. You must just learn to live with it." He closed his eyes again.

2 What are you thinking about now?

"But this is ridiculous," said Tonga. "No one can sit and talk with us tigers because we make so much noise. There must have been a mistake."

"A mistake!" said Sahr, sitting up. "No, no, no, I never make mistakes. Now go away." Sahr lay back down and closed his eyes once more.

After a few minutes Sahr opened one eye and saw Tonga still sitting patiently beside him.

"Shoo," said Sahr. "Go away."

Tonga lay down and, as he did, his coat of pipes made so much noise Sahr had to cover his ears. "I'm not going away until you do something about my coat," said Tonga.

Sahr sighed. "Oh, all right," he said. "I'll look it up."

He opened up the bottom of the tree and searched around. After several minutes he pulled out a large moss-covered book.

"It's really not fair that I have to do so much work," grumbled Sahr. "Not fair at all."

3 What are you thinking about now?

Tonga waited.

"Hmm-hmm-hmm," said Sahr. "This is going to take me quite a long time. Tiger does begin with *T*, you know. It will take me awhile to get there. You had better come back next week."

Tonga said nothing. He just waited.

"Oh, drats," said Sahr, who was really quite lazy. "Let's see. Cougars, leopards, lions. Ah, here we are— tigers. You can see for yourself—right beside 'tigers' it says 'pipes.'"

Tonga looked. "That says 'stripes'!" exclaimed Tonga. "Not 'pipes.'"

4 What do you think about Sahr's mistake?

"Oh, my stars," said Sahr. He looked more closely at his book. "So it does." He laughed. "My mistake. Oh dear. Well, we had better fix that."

Sahr snapped his fingers, and instantly Tonga's coat of pipes was gone. Instead, he had a beautiful coat of stripes. Tonga thanked Sahr, and he raced off to find his friends.

Sahr lay back down and closed his eyes. "I really must be more careful," he mumbled sleepily. "It's like the time I covered all those leopards with pots."

As for Tonga and the other tigers, they thoroughly enjoyed their new coats, and the jungle became a much quieter place to live.

5   What are you thinking about now?

Time to Write!

You just read a story about how tigers got their stripes.

• For this activity, you will write your own story to tell why an animal looks the way it does.

Prewriting

First, list three animals and your ideas about why they look the way they do.

Animal	Why the animal looks the way it does

Writing

Now, choose one animal. Use another sheet of paper to write your own story.

Thinking Along on Tests

You have been thinking along as you read. Now practice thinking along to help you answer test questions.

Read and Think

- Read each selection.
- Stop at each box and answer the question.
- Answer the questions at the end of each selection.

Why do bats have a bad name?

Bats have a bad name! Bats look scary to some people. Bats also can fly, but they are not birds. They are the only mammals that can fly. Some people are afraid that bats will get caught in their hair. Bats do not try to do that. Some people think bats will bite them. Bats almost never bite a person.

 1   What are you thinking about now?

One kind of bat is called a vampire bat. Vampire bats do bite. But they bite cattle, not people. There are stories about people who become vampires. These horror stories are fun for people who like to be scared. They are just made up. They are not real. The fear of make-believe human vampires has helped give bats a bad name.

During the day bats hang upside down from the top of caves or rock piles. Bats sleep during the day and come out at night. This is another reason people are afraid of bats. People think bad things about the dark and night. They think that bats must be bad.

2 What are you thinking about now?

In some areas, people have tried to get rid of bats. They closed the caves where bats live. Bats could not leave to find food. They died without food. Bats have had a bad time.

"So what?" you might say. "So people should not be afraid of bats. Why is that important?" The important thing is that bats help people in many ways.

Bats eat insects that harm crops and bite people. One bat can eat 1,000 mosquitoes in one hour! There is another good thing about bats. Bats that eat flowers help the flower make fruit. The bats also help move seeds to a new place to grow. Also, farmers use bat droppings, called guano, to help crops grow.

Today some people are trying to help bats. They want bats to eat insects. These people put bat houses in their yards. These houses have slots for the bats to climb in and sleep during the day. Some people turn on lights at night. They also plant flowers that bloom at night. Both of these attract moths and other insects that the bats like to eat. Bats also need water to drink. People make garden ponds for them.

It may take some time for everyone to understand that bats are not bad. It is important to spread the word about the good things that bats do.

3 What are you thinking about now?

Darken the circle for the correct answer.

1. The writer thinks that people should _____.
   - Ⓐ get rid of all bats
   - Ⓑ stop reading about vampires
   - Ⓒ learn to like bats
   - Ⓓ live in caves

2. Some people are afraid that bats will bite and _____.
   - Ⓐ get caught in their hair
   - Ⓑ eat too many insects
   - Ⓒ hurt their ponds
   - Ⓓ harm crops

3. One fact about bats is that they _____.
   - Ⓐ try to bite people
   - Ⓑ sleep during the day
   - Ⓒ are birds
   - Ⓓ cannot fly

4. Bats help people because they _____.
   - Ⓐ live only in caves
   - Ⓑ like to scare people
   - Ⓒ have to drink water
   - Ⓓ eat many insects

Write your answer on the lines below.

5. What is one way people can help bats?

_____

_____

_____

Why does a hiker need a mirror?

Ashton had asked his friend Harrison to
come along on his family's camping trip.
The boys decided by the campfire that they
would spend the next day hiking. Ashton
suggested that his sister Tamesha could go
along. Tamesha could see Harrison making
a face even in the dark. Her mom and dad
seemed to think it was a great idea.

The boys packed their backpacks before dark. They
wanted to get an early start the next morning. Dad
told Tamesha she could use the old pack he bought at
the army-navy store. Tamesha was not sure what to
take, so she left some of Dad's stuff in the bag.

---

1   What are you thinking about now?

On the trail, Tamesha tried to keep up. They were
climbing steep hills in places. Once or twice she got
behind. "Hurry up!" Harrison growled. "You could have
stayed at camp and gone fishing with your mom."

They stopped for lunch, and the boys pulled sandwiches out of their bags. "You did bring some food, didn't you?" Harrison said to Tamesha. He unwrapped his sandwich and winked at Ashton.

"No," Tamesha said. "I didn't think of that." She searched through Dad's backpack. She pulled a metal mirror out of a cloth. It caught the sun and shined in Harrison's eyes.

2 What are you thinking about now?

"Gee, whiz!" Harrison growled. "Why did you bring a mirror on a hike?" Then he reached for another sandwich in his pack. "Your mom said this is for you," he said, handing it to her.

They hiked for hours. Tamesha thought they were going in circles. Finally, Ashton stopped. "I'm lost," he said. "I don't have any idea which way leads back to camp."

"*We're* lost, you mean," Harrison said. "We'd better figure it out, though. The sun will go down in a couple of hours."

Tamesha was nervous. They were lost in the woods! Finally they came to the top of a bare hill where they could see a long way.

"Look!" Ashton yelled, pointing down at one valley. He could see his parents on a trail. They were looking for the hikers. The children began yelling to them. They could tell that they could not be heard.

Tamesha thought a minute. Then she pulled the mirror out of her dad's pack.

Harrison made an awful face. "Great!" he said. "What good will that do?"

Tamesha held the mirror so that it caught the sun and made bright flashes. Soon they could see Mom and Dad waving their arms at them.

"Sure glad you had that mirror, Tamesha," Harrison said, smiling.

 3 What are you thinking about now?

Darken the circle for the correct answer.

6. **How does Tamesha know that Harrison does not want her to go along?**

   (A) He makes a face.

   (B) He eats her sandwich.

   (C) He takes her mirror.

   (D) He smiles at her.

8. **Why were Mom and Dad out on the trail?**

   (A) They were looking for the mirror.

   (B) They knew Tamesha had no sandwich.

   (C) They thought the children were lost.

   (D) They were on their way home.

7. **Tamesha brought the mirror because _____.**

   (A) she wanted to look good

   (B) Ashton needed it

   (C) Harrison didn't like her having it

   (D) it was already in Dad's pack

9. **A good title for this story would be _____.**

   (A) Friendly Campers

   (B) Tamesha Saves the Day

   (C) Tamesha's Mistake

   (D) The Broken Mirror

Write your answer on the lines below.

10. **How do you think Tamesha feels at the end of the story?**

   _____

   _____

   _____

   _____

What do we know about Cliff Dwellers?

Do you know about the Cliff Dwellers? They are one of the great mysteries of the world. They built their homes into high, steep cliffs. Some ruins are over 2,000 feet above the floor of the valley below.

Many of these ruins are found in the southwestern United States. Here the four states Colorado, Utah, Arizona, and New Mexico meet. This area is called the "four corners." The most famous ruins are found on Mesa Verde. It is a high, flat-topped hill in Colorado.

No one knows for sure who built these cliff dwellings. Who were these people? Where did they come from? Where did they go? Many experts believe that these people were the ancestors of today's Pueblo Indians. The Pueblo call them the Anasazi.

1 What are you thinking about now?

These people probably first dug holes, or pits, to store supplies. Later they lined the pits with stones, put on roofs, and moved in. Then they began to build their homes on ledges in the sides of the cliffs. No one knows why they did this. Maybe they moved to be safe from enemies.

Some of these cliff buildings were four stories high. The bottom floor had no doors or windows. People used a ladder to enter through a hole in the ceiling. They could then pull the ladder in behind them.

 2   What are you thinking about now?

The cliff homes were built of stone and mud. One dwelling has over 200 rooms. It is called Cliff Palace. It had special rooms for keeping food and blankets for the winter.

There was a large room under the floor of the palace. It was the kiva (KEE vah). It was for special ceremonies, storytelling, and weaving. Only men could go down into the kiva. It had a deep, dark hole leading to what the people thought was the secret of life.

Women stayed above the kiva and made clay pots for cooking corn, squash, and beans. They grew these crops on the flat top of the hill above the dwelling. But this area could be very, very dry.

After about 300 years these people left their cliff homes. The reason is a mystery. Some experts believe there was too little rain, and the crops may have died.

Everything we know about the Cliff Dwellers we have guessed from the ruins of their homes. Yet the more we find, the more mysterious they seem.

---

3 What are you thinking about now?

Darken the circle for the correct answer.

11. The Cliff Dwellers are so mysterious because _____.

  Ⓐ they left no ruins

  Ⓑ little about them is known for certain

  Ⓒ they had no homes

  Ⓓ they grew no food

12. Some people believe the cliff dwellings were built to _____.

  Ⓐ get up above floods

  Ⓑ reach the sky

  Ⓒ be away from enemies

  Ⓓ find the secret of life

13. What is a mesa?

  Ⓐ a high flat-topped hill

  Ⓑ a hole in the ground

  Ⓒ something made of corn

  Ⓓ the story of the Anasazi

14. We have learned that the Cliff Palace _____.

  Ⓐ was in a valley

  Ⓑ was built of pots

  Ⓒ had no place for food

  Ⓓ had many rooms

Write your answer on the lines below.

15. Describe the cliff dwellings.

_____

_____

_____

_____

Acknowledgments

Grateful acknowledgment is made to the following authors and publishers for the use of copyrighted materials. Every effort has been made to obtain permission to use previously published material. Any errors or omissions are unintentional.

Abe Lincoln's Hat by Martha Brenner. Text copyright © 1994 by Martha Brenner. Illustrations copyright © 1994 by Donald Cook. Reprinted by arrangement with Random House, Inc.

Diego Rivera: An Artist's Life by Sarah Vázquez. Copyright © 1998 by Steck-Vaughn Company.

"Elsa's Pet" by Maureen Ash. Copyright © 1998 by Maureen Ash. First appeared in *Click* magazine, August 1998. Reprinted by permission of Maureen Ash.

Floss by Kim Lewis. Copyright © 1992 Kim Lewis. Reproduced by permission of Candlewick Press Inc., Cambridge, MA.

Gail Devers: A Runner's Dream by Katherine Mead. Copyright © 1998 by Steck-Vaughn Company.

A Look at Spiders by Jerald Halpern. Copyright © 1998 by Steck-Vaughn Company.

The Paper Bag Princess by Robert N. Munsch, illustrated by Michael Martchenko. Copyright © 1980 by Robert N. Munsch and Michael Martchenko. Reprinted by permission of Annick Press Ltd.

"Rocco's Yucky" by Linda Crotta Brennan. Reprinted by permission of LADYBUG magazine, November 1998, Vol. 9, No. 3, copyright © 1998 by Linda Crotta Brennan.

Save the River! by Sarah Glasscock. Copyright © 1998 by Steck-Vaughn Company.

"Some Jungles Are Noisier Than Others" by J. R. M. Vance. Copyright © 1995 by Highlights for Children, Inc., Columbus, Ohio. Reprinted by permission of Highlights for Children, Inc.

Whales: The Gentle Giants by Joyce Milton. Text copyright © 1989 by Joyce Milton. Illustrations copyright © by Alton Langford. Reprinted by arrangement with Random House, Inc.

"Wilbur Meets the Thing" by Caroline Coderre. Copyright © 1995 by Highlights for Children, Inc., Columbus, Ohio. Reprinted by permission of Highlights for Children, Inc.

Illustration Credits

Linda Kelen, 4, 28, 72, 106; Michael Martchenko, 6–12; Tadeusz Majewski, cover, 14–20; George Ulrich, cover, 22–26; Alton Langford, 30–40; Laura Jackson, 63, 64, 69, 136; Kim Lewis, 74–80; Donald Cook, 94–104; Esther Szegedy, cover, 108–112; D. R. Greenlaw, cover, 114–124; Maya Itzna-Brooks, cover, 126–130.

Photography Credits

Cover Sam Dudgeon; p.5 Rick Williams; p.29 Rick Williams; p.42 ©Francis G. Mayer/Corbis; p.43 ©PhotoDisc; p.44 ©Nik Wheeler/Corbis; p.45 ©PhotoDisc; p.46 Danny Lehman/©Corbis; p.47 CORBIS/Archivo Iconografico, S.A.; p.48-49(t) The Detroit Institute of the Arts; p.48(b) ©PhotoDisc; p.50 Danny Lehman/©Corbis; p.52 ©Rocky Jordan/Animals Animals; p.53 ©Chris Mattison; Frank Lane Picture Agency/Corbis; p.54 ©Paul Freed/Animals Animals; p.55 ©Hal Horwitz/Corbis; p.56 ©Donald Specker/Animals Animals; p.57 ©Patti Murray/Animals Animals; p.58 ©Anthony Bannister; ABPL/Corbis; p.59 ©C. W. Perkins/Animals Animals; p.60 ©Ronnie Kaufman/The Stock Market; p.67 ©Corel Photo Studios; p.73 Rick Williams; p.82 ©Gary M. Prior/Allsport; p.83 ©Mike Powell/Allsport; p.84 ©Focus on Sports; p.85 ©Mike Powell/Allsport; p.86 ©Bob Daemrich; p.87 ©Steve Powell/Allsport; p.89 ©Allsport; p.90 ©Simon Bruty/Allsport; p.91 ©David Cannon/Allsport; p.92 ©Gary M. Prior/Allsport; p.107 Rick Williams; p.132 ©Raymond A. Mendez/Animals Animals; p.134 ©Dalton, S. OSF/Animals Animals; p.140 ©PhotoDisc; p.142 CORBIS/Richard A. Cooke.